W9-AXU-818

Lee Bennett Hopkins

Lee Bennett Hopkins

A CHILDREN'S POET

AMY STRONG

FRANKLIN WATTS
A Division of Scholastic Inc.
New York Toronto London Auckland Sydney
Mexico City New Delhi Hong Kong
Danbury, Connecticut

Photographs © 2003: Reprinted with permission from Bank Street College of Education: 44; Reprinted by permission of Boyds Mills Press, Inc.: 88 (*Been to Yesterdays: Poems of a Life*, by Lee Bennett Hopkins, © 1995, published by Wordsong); Brown Brothers/Baroff: 11, 12; Corbis Images: 60 (James L. Amos), 56 (Archivo Iconografico, S.A.), 16, 29, 50 top, 50 bottom, 54 (Vince Streano); de Grummond Children's Literature Collection, The University of Southern Mississippi: 75 (by permission of Curtis Brown Ltd.), 80, 84; Reprinted by permission of Harper Collins Children's Books, a division of Harper Collins Publishers: 64 (*Hoofbeats, Claws & Rippled Fins: Creature Poems*, edited by Lee Bennett Hopkins, jacket art © 2002 by Stephen Alcorn, All rights reserved); Kean University: 38, 65, 68; Courtesy of Lee Bennett Hopkins: 6, 8 bottom, 8 top, 10, 14, 18, 20, 24, 25, 30, 34, 35, 39 top, 39 bottom, 77, 78, 79, 82, 85, 86; Nick Romanenko: cover, 2, 42, 92, 94, 96, 97, 99; Stephen Alcorn: 91; The Image Works/Topham: 59; TimePix/Robert W. Kelley: 46.

Library of Congress Cataloging-in-Publication Data

Strong, Amy.

Lee Bennett Hopkins : a children's poet / by Amy Strong.
       p. cm. — (Great life stories)
Summary: Looks at the life and work of children's poet Lee Bennett Hopkins, who has been a full-time writer for over twenty-five years.
    Includes bibliographical references and index.
    ISBN 0-531-12315-4
    1. Hopkins, Lee Bennett—Juvenile literature. 2. Poets, American—20th century—Biography—Juvenile literature. 3. Poetry—Authorship—Juvenile literature. [1. Hopkins, Lee Bennett. 2. Authors, American.]   I. Title.   II. Series.

PS3558.O63544Z87 2003
813'.54—dc21

                                                          200300463

Contents

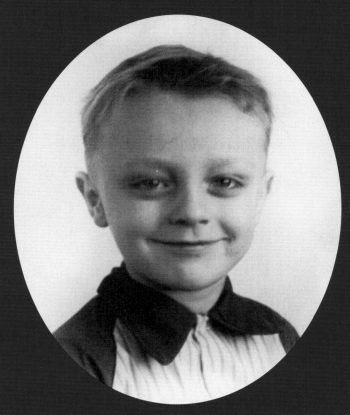

For Lee Bennett Hopkins, his childhood would
prove to be a source of some of his greatest work.

ONE

Growing Up

One of today's most important children's poets, Lee Bennett Hopkins, got his start in the rough-and-tumble city of Scranton, Pennsylvania, on April 13, 1938. Little did his parents know that their first child would grow up to become a strong creative force and a lifelong advocate of poetry.

Lee's parents lived at 806 Philo Street in a small, two-story colonial house with white siding and a covered front porch. They didn't have any land—it was definitely a city house. The front yard looked more like a patch of dirt than a manicured lawn, but they lived in it quite comfortably. Lee was born in that house.

ABOVE: This is the house at 806 Philo Street where Lee was born.

BELOW: This photograph shows Lee's mother, Gertrude, on her wedding day, April 11, 1936.

Lee's father, Leon, was a police officer. Little is known about Leon's background or family history. He grew up in Pennsylvania and came from a working-class family. He was a tall, imposing man, with a long, narrow face and a leathery complexion. His dark hair was cut short above his ears, and his high forehead accentuated his dark eyes and heavy eyebrows. When he smiled, long dimples marked his cheeks.

Lee's mother, Gertrude, was also born and raised in Pennsylvania. She was a trim and active woman with a zest for life. Her curly dark hair was often pulled back with barrettes to keep it away from her face. The members of the Hopkins family were by no means wealthy during the years they lived in Scranton, but they were getting by well enough, so Lee's mother didn't need to work outside the home.

Gertrude's mother, Lena Thomas, became an important and positive role model for Lee in his young life. He absolutely adored his grandmother and spent as much time as he could with her, especially in the summers. Lee recalls his grandmother bouncing him on her knee and reciting nursery rhymes, which was his first introduction to poetry. She worked as the superintendent of an apartment building and provided Lee with a feeling of stability.

Gertrude's father, George Thomas, worked in the Pennsylvania coal mines, a common profession for men in Scranton, Pennsylvania, during the first half of the twentieth century. Scranton had been a wealthy city at one time, primarily because it produced more coal, iron, and steel than just about any other city in the world. As a girl, Gertrude would walk along the railroad tracks and pick up stray pieces of coal that had fallen off the transport trains. Coal was so precious at that time that individual pieces could be sold for a small profit.

Coal mining was a harsh, dirty, and dangerous business. Lee's grandfather would head into the mines every morning wearing a hard hat

Radio Days

During the Great Depression, families had very little money to spend on entertainment outside the home. Lee's parents loved to sit by the radio in the evenings and listen to the music of Jan Garber's band. One of the lead singers in the band was named Lee Bennett. Lee's mother thought to herself, "When we have our first child, we're going to name it Lee Bennett." And that's precisely what they did.

fixed with a flashlight. He and his fellow workers whacked away at the coal with picks and drills, filled up containers, and dragged the coal-filled containers out of the mine. Tunnels and shafts leading into and out of the mine were sometimes very steep, so the miners were forced to crawl up and down with great care. Seams of coal could be rather narrow or shallow, and the miners might work stooped over or on their hands and knees for hours on end. In the early 1800s, children were employed to work in the mines because they were smaller and they could more easily squeeze into tight spaces.

Stones and pieces of coal tumbled down on the workers' heads. Coal dust fouled the air, forcing the miners to breathe unsafe air all day long. At times, water would seep into the mine shafts and the working conditions became very cold and damp. Worst of all, when coal is mined, it releases methane gas, which can cause a large explosion once exposed to fresh air. Despite these difficult working conditions,

Lee's grandfather, George Thomas, worked as a coal miner, a difficult and dangerous profession.

coal mining remained the dominant industry in Scranton for several decades.

Once the Great Depression hit in 1929, all of that changed. It was the worst economic slump ever seen in the United States, and its effects were felt all over the world. The stock market crashed, banks ran out of money, farmers went bankrupt, and factories had to fire many of their workers in order to survive. Thirteen million people in the United States lost their jobs.

By the time Lee was born, in 1938, parts of Pennsylvania had suffered a whopping 40 percent unemployment rate. Scranton still looked the same as it always had, with its imposing brick factories and sleek railroad lines, but its core had been gutted. The estimated population of close to 150,000 began to dwindle rapidly as a sizable proportion of its citizens moved to other towns and cities seeking better employment opportunities. It wouldn't be long before Lee's family would join the exodus.

This photograph shows the city of Scranton, Pennsylvania, around the time that Lee was born.

EARLY CHILDHOOD DURING WAR

The first seven years of Lee's life coincided with one of the most devastating events in modern history, World War II. Between 1939 and 1945, Germany, led by Adolf Hitler and the Nazi Party, began a series of invasions on surrounding European countries, including Poland, Denmark, Norway, France, and Belgium, among others. The U.S. president was conflicted about whether to get involved in a war overseas, but all ambivalence vanished on December 7, 1941, when Japan bombed Pearl Harbor, a military base in Hawaii. President Franklin D. Roosevelt declared that moment as "a date which will live in infamy." The war wouldn't end for nearly four more years, and millions of soldiers and civilians would be wounded and killed.

Despite its enormous impact on world events, World War II had little effect on the Hopkins family. Lee's father did not fight in the war, although Lee's uncles served in the military. Lee's mother put an American

This photograph shows Scranton during World War II, a time when many types of goods were rationed.

Stars in the Windows

Lee also remembers that families would hang stars in their windows to indicate that a loved one was in the war. The number of stars corresponded to the number of family members in the service. A flag with one star meant one person from the family was serving in the military.

flag in their window to show support for the cause and made rag balls to bring in a little extra income. Lee was just a child at the time of World War II, but he does remember one small way the war affected his life. During wartime, the federal government rationed certain products that were in short supply, such as sugar, meat, coffee, rubber, and gas. For Lee, the rationing of sugar meant that he had to stand in line for much longer than usual to buy one bag of Easter jelly beans.

Lee's younger brother, Donald, was born in the midst of World War II on August 9, 1941, and his little sister, Donna Lea, was born on July 16, 1947. All three babies were born in the same house in Scranton, all in the same bed, all on a Wednesday.

After the war ended, the economy in Scranton took a nosedive. The demand for coal, steel, and iron wasn't what it used to be, and Lee's parents could see that good job opportunities in the city were rapidly declining. Some of Lee's relatives had recently moved to Newark, New Jersey, and they all reported that the town was thriving. So Lee's parents packed up their three children and moved to Newark. Lee later wrote a poem about the experience:

PACK

the boxes
into the car,
pile the dishes,
load in the clothes,
squeeze in the
pots and pans,
our two radios—
can't waste a space—
everything goes.

This is a portrait of the Hopkins family: (clockwise left to right) Donna Lea, Leon, Gertrude, Lee, and Donald.

Crowd in the Mama,
the Daddy,
the sister,
jam in the brother,
make room for my toes—
can't waste a space—
everything goes.

Bundle the memories
We're moving today
from
Scranton, PA
to
Newark, NJ.

The move to Newark would bring new challenges for the Hopkins family.

TWO

The Man of the House

When they first arrived in Newark, Lee and his family moved into an apartment on Court Street with his aunt, uncle, and three cousins. Four adults and six children all lived together in the same small space. As soon as Lee's family got settled, they found an apartment of their own, but it wasn't much of an improvement. They moved into a dark and gloomy basement apartment that was so far underground, when Lee gazed outside his small apartment windows, all he could see were people's legs passing by. Lee's parents worked as superintendents of the building. From there, the family moved to a railroad flat in another section of Newark. Leon took a job doing construction, while Gertrude picked up odd jobs whenever possible.

Living in cramped quarters was made more difficult because Lee's mother struggled with a drinking problem. She could function quite well in society and she managed to hold down a number of jobs, but she drank too much just about every day of her adult life. Lee recalls, "My childhood was totally screwed up. I don't think I ever saw a moment when my mother was sober."

Lee tried everything he could think of to get his mother to quit drinking. He pleaded with her and poured her liquor down the toilet— anything to get her attention. Nothing worked. Many children who grow up with an alcoholic parent struggle to adjust and cope, but Lee managed extremely well. He focused first and foremost on survival and took comfort in the knowledge that his mother loved him deeply and wanted the very best for him.

Lee became quite protective of his younger siblings. As the oldest child, he felt responsible for taking care of his younger brother and sister.

As the oldest child, Lee felt very protective of his siblings.

When he was only ten or eleven years old, Lee took over many of the household chores, helped Donald and Donna Lea with homework, and put them to bed at night.

Lee wanted to protect both of his siblings from the whirlwind going on all around them. He became especially protective of Donna Lea, as she was nine years younger than he was. As she got older, he would take her into New York City to visit museums or see a show at the theater.

THE END OF CHILDHOOD

The relationship between Lee's parents had been a tumultuous one since they moved to New Jersey and it was obvious to all of the kids that something had to change. They were constantly fighting—long, drawn-out fights. Both parents threatened divorce, but neither one dared take the final step toward severing the ties until one day that Lee would never forget.

One afternoon, Lee walked into the family's apartment and couldn't believe his eyes. The walls were bare, the furniture was gone, and the entire place was cleaned out. No note from his father, no farewell hugs—just a vast, empty space. Several days later, Lee walked down the street and saw where their furniture had gone. His father had sold it all to the owner of a nearby furniture store.

Little did they know, Lee, Donna Lea, and Donald would not see their father again for more than thirty years.

Like Lee's mother, Aunt Doris struggled to support her family.

Once Leon left the family, Gertrude and the children were nearly penniless. Leon had brought in an income as a police officer in Scranton and had worked good jobs in construction while the family lived in Newark. All that time, Gertrude had stayed at home or worked at an occasional odd job. They had no savings and no money coming in, so they did what they had to do. The entire family moved back in with Lee's Aunt Doris and her three children on Court Street. Lee says, "Being the oldest of the six [children], I had to keep the house running fairly smoothly while Mom and Aunt Doris worked long, arduous hours to support us."

It wasn't long before the two families realized this cramped housing situation would not work in the long term. Gertrude and Doris both applied for separate apartments in a new, low-income housing project in Newark. Doris was accepted in the Kretchmer

Projects, and Lee's family took an apartment in the much older Seth Boyden Projects, several blocks away. The tiny apartment had just a few rooms, including a living room, kitchen, and two bedrooms. Lee and Donald slept in one bedroom, while Donna Lea and Gertrude shared the other. Lee recalls, "The neighborhood was mixed ethnically; the one thing we all had in common was acute poverty."

All of these changes helped to form Lee's personality. He had become fiercely independent and was determined to get himself and his siblings through the tough times. Despite all of the chaos and turmoil, he always remained hopeful about the future. Perhaps his tendency to embrace optimism came from his mother, who always kept a cheerful disposition, even when the family navigated the roughest seas. She taught Lee to have faith in what tomorrow would bring.

In many ways, that optimism and zest for life may have been Gertrude's greatest gift to her children. Despite the poverty and the family hardships Lee endured during those early years in Newark, he delights in recalling the simple pleasures of his youth. He says, "As a child I loved the simple things about life—gum, the movies, hydrants and daydreaming while riding on a swing. No one ever told my brother, sister, my friends or me that we were poor. These were things that we all did and loved— they were part of our childhood, they were what life was all about."

The street, with all of its energy, chaos, and great rush of humanity, was a place where Lee felt at home. Lee's recollections of those years are nostalgic and heartfelt, filled with loving memories of his mother's generosity and determination to provide her children with everything they needed.

GETTING BY

Forced to bring up her three children as a single parent, Gertrude became very creative about earning enough money to continue paying the rent, buying clothes, bringing home food, and meeting her children's needs.

Even when they had a stable roof over their heads, the family members often fell behind on their bill at the local grocery store. When the family fell too far behind on their tab, Gertrude would ask Lee to do all of the shopping. It was not easy for Lee to do the family's shopping when its tab had grown too high. The man behind the counter, usually so friendly and kind, became dour and cold. When Lee approached the counter, he braced himself for the inevitable confrontation.

"When is your mother going to pay her bill?" the grocer would ask. "You tell your mother that I want to see her. I can't go on giving you credit if you don't pay up your bill."

The man never went so far as to embarrass Lee in front of other customers—he would take care to pull Lee aside—but it almost didn't matter. Lee's humiliation was complete, whether or not others witnessed it.

When Gertrude paid off their tab, Lee felt jubilant, back in the good graces of the grocer. But that euphoria often disappeared within a matter of weeks when they again went into debt.

Lee might have been spared this embarrassment if his mother had been willing to accept outside help. Gertrude was not willing to take that step. She wanted to remain self-sufficient and support her family through work, without accepting any form of charity. She believed that food stamps were for people who couldn't find jobs or for older people who were unable to work. As long as she was able-bodied, she would support her family the best way she knew how. As it happened, the best way she knew how involved breaking the law. Gertrude became a thief.

A DANGEROUS PROFESSION

Gertrude never kept a job for very long, always moving from one workplace to the next. At each new job, she found a way to take things from her employer. When she worked at a department store, she stole clothes for her children. When she worked for a meatpacking plant, she stole meat to bring home for dinner. When she worked at a five-and-ten-cent store during the busy holiday season, she stole Christmas ornaments.

Cost of Living

Compared to prices today, the cost of many things in the 1950s may seem incredibly low. The average price for a house was $16,000, and a Ford automobile cost $1,500 to $2,000. Filling up the gas tank of a car cost only 20 cents per gallon. However, to really understand what these prices meant to most people in 1951, it is important to remember that the average annual income was only around $3,700.

While her methods were unusual, Gertrude tried to do everything she could to provide for her children.

Occasionally, she recruited an accomplice: her young son, Lee. When Lee's mother worked at the five-and-ten-cent store, for example, she wanted to have certain things from the store for her family but didn't earn enough money to afford them. In one of Lee's poems about his childhood, he describes his mother's longing for a butter dish from Woolworth's that cost just 29 cents. At any rate, as an employee of the store, Gertrude couldn't simply walk out with the objects that she wanted to steal, so she devised another plan.

Lee would enter the store where his mother worked and pretend that he didn't know her. After selecting several items from the shelves, he would bring them to his mother's register. Gertrude would ring up his purchases, adding a few more items for good measure, and then pretend to take his money. He would quickly leave the store with a bag full of stolen goods.

One Christmas, Lee's mother stole a huge supply of ornaments, and their tree just

Lee and Donald pose with Santa at Christmastime. Their mother tried to make the holidays special one year by shoplifting decorations and ornaments.

sagged under the weight of all the balls and candy canes and tinsel and ornaments of all shapes and sizes. Instead of three wise men, the family's Christmas tree had eighteen: five carrying gold, six carrying myrrh, and seven carrying frankincense.

Gertrude was so successful as a shoplifter that her children never felt disadvantaged in any way. In fact, Lee very consciously feels that they were quite well cared for. He says, "I was never disadvantaged. My mother was a thief, a shoplifter—so we had everything! At times there was so much meat in the refrigerator we gave it to neighbors."

With what she took, Gertrude was incredibly generous. If she ever had more than the family needed, she would give some away to the neighbors, or, occasionally, she would barter. She might give her neighbor some boiled ham, and the neighbor would bake her a cake. Or she would leave the milkman some cold cuts, and he would leave her a few extra eggs or an extra jug of milk. Somehow, Gertrude always managed to provide everything her children needed. Above all, she gave them unconditional love, and that fed their hearts and souls for a lifetime.

Mama Says

Lee's mother once said, "I never remember the Three Wise Men saying anything. The reason they were called the Wise Men is because they kept their mouths shut."

THREE

Saved His Life

Lee's childhood experiences were often difficult, but they made him strong and independent. Gertrude instilled precisely the right combination of values to encourage Lee's later success in life: imagination, optimism, and dogged determination.

Lee never expected, during his adolescence, that he would accomplish anything extraordinary, certainly not in the lofty realm of poetry. As a teenager, he focused, first and foremost, on survival.

In one of his poems, Lee recalls the day his father walked out on the family. It felt like a "branch was slashed from our family tree." Lee had no way of knowing then that his early experiences of loss would, many decades later, provide inspiration for some of his most beloved poems. In the meantime, he filled his days by working odd jobs, being fiercely protective toward his younger brother and sister, and spending time with friends and a girlfriend whom he adored.

AN INSPIRATIONAL TEACHER

When Lee was in junior high school, "I was fourteen and in eighth grade when my teacher, Mrs. Ethel Kite McLaughlin, saw something in this mixed up child, and spun my world around." Lee's teacher believed in him, took his work seriously, and introduced him to the beauty and power of language and theater. To a young boy brought up in a culture of poverty, divorce, and crime, Mrs. McLaughlin's encouragement was incredibly meaningful.

She introduced Lee to the theater and encouraged him to see plays whenever he could find the time and money. A nearby theater called the Paper Mill Playhouse, in Millburn, New Jersey, was doing a production of *Kiss Me, Kate* (a famous musical based on William Shakespeare's comedy *The Taming of the Shrew*). A balcony seat cost $1.20, plus the round-trip bus fare of 30 cents. Lee recalls, "This was 1952. I could never scrape up that amount of money. Things were so bad [at home] that our telephone was taken out and gas and electric shut off because we couldn't pay the bills."

Inspired by his teacher, Lee entered a newspaper competition. The *Newark Star-Ledger* sponsored a contest called "Babies Are Bright" that asked readers to send in a baby photo with a clever caption. Lee entered a photo of his cousin, wrote a short caption, and won $10—he gave $8

On Broadway

On the weekends, Lee took buses into New York City and headed for the theater capital of the world: Broadway. He didn't have enough money to purchase tickets for Broadway productions, but he found a way around that. Lee would figure out approximately when the intermission would be and then would sneak into the theater and watch the second half. Lee jokingly says that, as a teenager, he saw the second half of nearly every musical showing on Broadway.

to his mother and kept the $2 so he could go out to see his first play. His seat was in the very last row, but he loved the performance and described it as a "thrilling experience that showed me there was more to life than the [housing] projects." Excited by the production, Lee began to borrow records of Broadway musicals from the public library. He would sing along to all the words and remained a fan of the theater for the rest of his life.

Mrs. McLaughlin also encouraged Lee to read plays and other forms of fiction. Lee had never cultivated any interest in reading, except for the few books that he found, literally, in the trash. In his apartment complex, he would occasionally scavenge around in the dumbwaiter, where his neighbors left their garbage, to see if there was anything salvageable. Every now and then, he would find a comic book, a movie magazine, or a detective story.

Mrs. McLaughlin encouraged Lee to read classic novels. The first full novel he ever read was Louisa May Alcott's beloved classic, *Little*

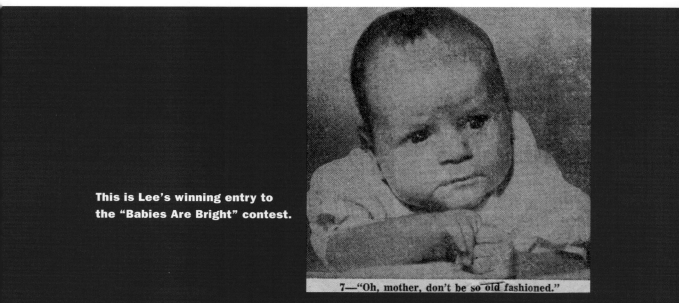

This is Lee's winning entry to the "Babies Are Bright" contest.

7—"Oh, mother, don't be so old fashioned."

Women. It's the story of a mother who raises her four daughters, Meg, Jo, Beth, and Amy, entirely on her own. The family is not especially well off financially and had its fair share of heartaches, but it is wonderfully happy and harmonious. The family's home always seems to be full of high spirits, laughter, and love. Recalling that first novel, Lee says, "When I got to the last page I turned back to the beginning and started reading it again. This went on for about a year. I thought, *this is the book for me. This is the family I never had.*"

A CLOSE CALL

When Lee was in his teens, he met and fell in love with a young woman named Evelyn. Both were great enthusiasts of roller skating, an extremely popular sport in the 1950s. They would meet at the roller rink and skate for hours at a time.

An American Snapshot

While Lee was discovering the world of books and theater in 1952, there was a lot happening in the world around him. People were flocking to see the movie musical *Singin' in the Rain* and the western *High Noon*. The musical *The King and I* won the 1952 Tony Award for best musical play. One of Ernest Hemingway's most popular books, *The Old Man and the Sea*, was published. In sports, the New York Yankees beat the Brooklyn Dodgers to win the World Series.

Although they were very close and very happy together, Evelyn kept a part of herself closed up. There were a number of things Lee didn't know about her family, her background, or her private life. In particular, Lee didn't know that Evelyn had been seeing another guy.

The other man was an ex-Marine, who was rough, unpredictable, and extremely jealous. Although Evelyn's relationship with the ex-Marine had become very rocky and she planned to end it, the time never felt quite right. She feared his temper and his dangerous, unhealthy attachment to her. The minute Evelyn mentioned her other friends to him, he became aggressive, insisting that she was "his" and that she couldn't go out with anybody else.

As much as she tried, Evelyn couldn't make her ex-boyfriend understand that she wasn't a piece of property that he owned but a free individual who had her own thoughts and her own life, apart from him.

One day at the skating rink, Lee made a date with Evelyn for the following Saturday night. They were going to get together at the skating rink. Lee very much looked forward to it. On the day of their date, he came down with strep throat and was forced to call her up and cancel. Little did he know that his case of strep throat would save his life.

The same night Lee and Evelyn were supposed to meet, the ex-Marine sought her out, furious with jealousy and determined to get revenge. He forced Evelyn to get into his car and drove it into her family's garage. He closed the door to the garage, locked himself and Evelyn in the car, and left the motor running all night long. By morning, both Evelyn and her ex-boyfriend were dead of carbon monoxide poisoning.

A Historic Decision

About a month after Lee's sixteenth birthday, the Supreme Court of the United States made a landmark decision making the practice of segregation on the basis of race in public schools illegal. While many school systems, such as Lee's, were already allowing all children to attend the same schools, some areas still maintained separate schools for African American students and white students. This practice had been considered legal as long as there were "separate but equal" schools for African American students. The Supreme Court decided that educational segregation violated the equal protection clause of the Fourteenth Amendment, which requires states to grant "equal protection of the laws" to all people.

When the police investigated the deaths, they came across a suicide note left behind by the ex-boyfriend. The note claimed that he planned to kill himself, Evelyn, and Lee via carbon monoxide poisoning. If Lee had met up with Evelyn that night, he would have been dead by the next morning.

On his sixteenth birthday, Lee attended Evelyn's funeral.

ALWAYS A SURVIVOR

After Evelyn's death, Lee focused his energies on helping his family. Leon was long gone, completely out of touch with the family. It was up to Lee to take whatever odd jobs he could find to bring in extra money.

The jobs kept him busy and brought in some income, but they held their own unexpected challenges. Once, while working at a small grocery store, Lee was downstairs in the cellar putting away empty bottles. When he walked up the staircase and into the store, he saw a man holding a gun to the store manager's head. The manager gave the burglar all the money in the cash register, and the burglar fled immediately. Lee was terrified by the ordeal, suddenly all too aware of his own vulnerability in the store, but he just couldn't quit. He needed the money.

All of his energy went into working at jobs in which he could bring home money for the family, and by the end of the day, he was usually far too exhausted to keep up with his schoolwork. Besides, school had always been a bit boring for Lee. He had grown up in a home where there were no rules and found it very difficult to adjust to the strict rules he endured at school all day long. His mother never told him when to go to bed or when to be home in the evenings. Even when Lee returned

Lee enjoys some time in the kitchen in December of 1954.

home after a late night out, he rarely made it home before his mother did. Rules were just not a part of the family's life.

No one walked into Lee's bedroom early in the morning to wake him up, help him get out of bed, make him eat a healthy breakfast, and get him to catch the school bus on time. Gertrude slept late or went off to work early, and it was up to the three kids to get themselves up and ready for school. Many mornings, Lee would wake up and search his mind for a reason to go to school. Many mornings, he couldn't come up with a good reason.

When Lee did attend school, it was tiresome for him to be told what to do all day long. Being required to adhere to a schedule of classes seemed far too strict. Truth be told, he cut classes at least as often as he attended them. Predictably, he never did especially well in his classes. The accumulation of missed days forced him to fall behind in nearly every subject.

Lee recalls, "There was little I liked about high school and little that I learned. I couldn't care less about the whole experience. It was rote

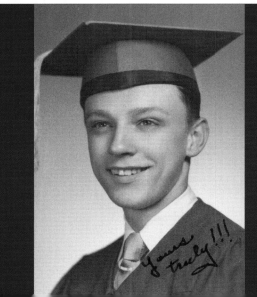

Lee graduated high school, ready to start the next chapter of his life.

learning personified. Any attempt at being creative was shunned. It was the school of memorization and giving back the facts." Lee does remember enjoying some of his English classes, but he despised mathematics and failed algebra not once, but twice.

Despite his feelings about the dull routine of high school, Lee wanted to go to college to follow a dream. He wanted to become a teacher and change the lives of students, as Mrs. McLaughlin had changed his.

FOUR

Becoming a Teacher

Not a single member of Lee's immediate family had ever graduated from college, but Lee was determined to be the first. Although he never enjoyed high school, his mission to become a teacher inspired him to continue his education and prepare for a career. Despite his mediocre high-school grades, he was admitted to Newark State Teachers College (now called Kean University) in 1956. Since the school was located in Newark, and after two years moved to nearby Union, he continued to live at home while attending classes.

Once enrolled, Lee realized just how far behind he had fallen in basic subjects. All of those days he cut class in high school finally caught up with him, and it soon became obvious that college-level work was going to be a struggle. For the first two years, he spent most of his time playing catch-up. He took remedial math and other basic, introductory-level courses just to gain a solid foundation in academics.

Lee still had to work after school to help pay for his tuition and fees. Lee remembers it being a very hectic time. "I remember one year leaving the Union campus each day at 3:00 P.M., taking a bus from Union to Elizabeth, changing on to another for Newark, and walking several blocks to an office where I did typing and clerical work from 3:45 to 5:30. From 5:30 to 6:00 I had time to grab a hamburger and Coke . . . before going to work in a large supermarket until 9:30 P.M., and then go back home via the bus to study until I fell asleep." During his last year of college, Lee worked the night shift at a supermarket warehouse, from midnight until 7:00 A.M. He ate his lunch at 3:00 A.M.

When Lee decided to major in teaching, the entire academic landscape changed for him. He soared. Suddenly, the course work seemed interesting, relevant, and worthwhile. He learned teaching methods and child psychology, and eagerly prepared for a career as a teacher.

Despite his heavy work schedule, Lee was involved in many different activities in college, such as the Norms Theater Guild

Lee poses for photographs with his mother and his grandparents on graduation day.

His grades improved steadily in the last two years of college, and he went from a mediocre student to well above average.

Lee was driven by the idea that maybe he could have an impact on kids, even change their lives, in the same way that Mrs. McLaughlin had an impact on him in the eighth grade.

During his senior year, Lee applied for an elementary teaching position at a public school in Fair Lawn, New Jersey. The school's superintendent agreed to interview Lee for the position. During the interview, the superintendent did his best to find out what kinds of ideas this new, young teacher might bring to the classroom. He handed Lee a book of matches and said, "This is all you have to teach with for the first three months in a sixth-grade classroom. What would you do?"

Lee instantly came alive with suggestions, covering everything from the invention of fire to mass advertising. The superintendent interrupted Lee's nonstop flow of ideas by standing up, offering a handshake, and exclaiming, "Welcome to Fair Lawn. You will be teaching the sixth grade in September."

Fair Lawn, a suburban, middle-class public school, held much more promise than the inner-city schools Lee had attended growing up. The atmosphere was more relaxed and tranquil. The school was a brand-new, beautiful, one-level building situated on several acres of land. Lee recalls, "When I saw the room I was assigned to I gasped. I had never seen a classroom like this in my entire life. It was huge, light, airy. Everything was sparkling new, supplies unlimited." Lee knew at once that teaching would be his life. He loved the kids, their excitement about learning, and his own natural ability to inspire and instill hope.

After teaching sixth grade for three years, Lee became the school's "resource teacher," which meant he selected and organized all the materials available to the school's elementary teachers. It was a job that called for great imagination and creativity, and Lee was more than up to the challenge. Lee says, "I worked with, and for, every teacher in the plant from kindergarten through grade six, a total of twelve faculty members. In addition to booking field trips, teaching special lessons, working with various groups from slow-learners to the gifted, I provided the resources for all subject areas. All a teacher had to do was say, 'I'm doing a unit on ancient Egypt.' I would then get everything I could find on the subject— films, filmstrips, photographs, maps, vertical files, trade books, human resources when I could find them, and tie-in a visit to the Metropolitan

Creating a Library

When Lee first began his job as resource teacher, his school had no library. Lee told the principal, "We need a library." She explained that the school had no room for one. Lee replied, "Yes we do!" He had discovered a tiny room near the school's gym that held only a few janitorial supplies. They cleaned out the room and filled it with books in no time.

Museum of Art in New York City to culminate the unit. I put everything on a rolling cart and wheeled it into the classroom. Entire resources were there waiting to be used by a most thankful teacher."

In one of his more inspired moments, Lee came up with the idea of using poetry to help children who have reading problems. The precise moment of inspiration came when he stumbled across a slim volume of poetry called *Whispers and Other Poems* by Myra Cohn Livingston. The poems were simple, easy to read, and well crafted. The poet set moods and shared moments of everyday childhood experiences, such as going to the zoo and riding on a merry-go-round.

As Lee recalls the flash of inspiration, he says, "*Whispers* led me to delve into the world of poetry for children. I searched and found, devoured and shared works with my students by David McCord, John Ciardi, Eve Merriam, poets who were being published in the late 1950s and 1960s."

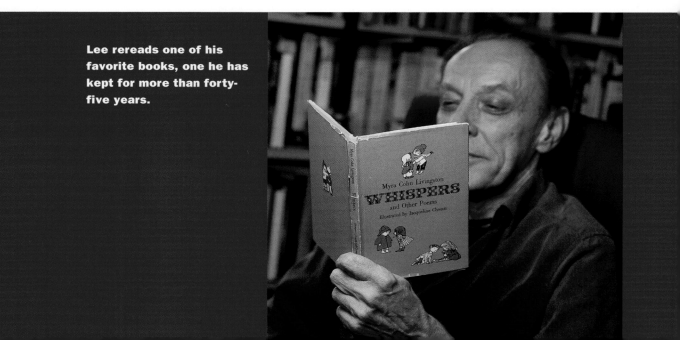

Lee rereads one of his favorite books, one he has kept for more than forty-five years.

An Avid Book Collector

Along with his copy of Myra Cohn Livingston's book of poetry, Lee has collected hundreds of books on poetry and children's literature over the years. His collection includes signed first editions of poetry books by Carl Sandburg and Shel Silverstein.

His idea took off immediately. Poetry became an important part of the elementary-education curriculum at Fair Lawn. Lee says, "Poetry became 'the thing.' I used it in every way possible—in every subject area. Mother Goose rhymes served to create mathematical word problems; Carl Sandburg's 'Arithmetic' was read before mathematics lessons; a holiday wouldn't go by without sharing a Valentine's Day, Halloween, or Christmas poem."

Lee still has his original copy of Myra Cohn Livingston's book of poetry. He bought it for $2.25 more than forty-five years ago and considers it one of the most important investments he has ever made.

ONE TINY FAVOR

The same year that Lee began teaching sixth grade, Bank Street College of Education in New York City began a pilot study that compared inner-city schools with suburban schools, and the college used Fair Lawn as its sample suburban school. One afternoon, the principal, Mrs. Haenechen, asked Lee to come to her office. She told him, "I've been in

With the help of his school's principal, Lee was able to attend Bank Street College.

this business a long, long time and I think you are one of the best teachers I've ever seen." Mrs. Haenechen was a tough person who rarely doled out compliments to any of her staff. "I think you should get your master's degree," she said.

Although Lee loved the idea, he knew that his bank account would never support a move like that. He only made $4,600 a year, and a sizable proportion of that money went toward his sister's schooling. The Newark public schools had become too dangerous for Donna Lea to feel safe in them, so she had enrolled in a parochial school, and Lee helped cover the costs. In fact, Lee hardly had enough money to buy new clothes or furniture for his apartment. Mrs. Haenechen was sympathetic to Lee's situation, but she was also completely determined to get him into a master's degree program.

The next day, the principal called Lee back into her office and said, "I think you should get your master's degree at Bank Street College of Education in New York."

Lee quickly did the math in his head, adding up tuition, fees, and subway fares back and forth to New York City. Lee thought it was impossible.

Mrs. Haenechen, however, had found a way. In just a single day, she had arranged for Bank Street College to give Lee a full scholarship. Lee later found out that his principal had more or less threatened several administrators at Bank Street, saying that if they wouldn't grant her this "one tiny favor," she would be forced to cancel the entire pilot study between Bank Street College and Fair Lawn.

Lee went on to receive his master's degree from Bank Street College in 1964. Just as he was finishing his master's degree, Bank Street College decided to open a learning resource center in the heart of Harlem, at 125th Street and Park Avenue. The administrators at Bank Street College interviewed Lee for the position of consultant, and they

War in Vietnam Expands

While Lee was starting a new chapter in his life, the Vietnam War began to escalate. After two U.S. destroyers had reportedly been attacked by North Vietnamese torpedo boats, President Lyndon Baines Johnson retaliated by ordering air strikes and pushing Congress to pass the Gulf of Tonkin Resolution. This resolution gave President Johnson increased powers for responding to attacks on U.S. military forces and enabled the United States to become more involved in the Vietnam War. By 1968, there would be more than half a million U.S. soldiers in Vietnam.

The work of Langston Hughes has been an important influence on Lee.

were impressed with his knowledge of African American history and literature. They hired him to work on a project called "Searchlight on Intelligence," which was designed to help talented African American children get into upward-bound programs, at a starting salary of $8,500. Although Lee was sorry to leave Fair Lawn, he couldn't pass up this opportunity to work with kids in Harlem. He reveled in the opportunity to help kids who faced so many of the same problems he had known growing up in Newark.

A FAVORITE POET

Because Harlem was a predominantly black section of New York City, Lee wanted to introduce students to the works of African American poets as much as possible. When he first discovered Langston Hughes's book of poetry for children, *The Dream Keeper and Other Poems*, it was a revelation. Lee fell in love with the poetry, and Hughes became a permanent part of his own career.

Langston Hughes was a wonderful poet who contributed greatly to a literary and cultural movement called the Harlem Renaissance. His poetry focused on city life, the streets of Harlem, the hearts and minds of African Americans, the vibrancy of black culture, the rhythm and blues of jazz musicians, and more. Growing up as an African American in the 1920s and 1930s, Langston Hughes suffered the effects of racism in American culture, but he was determined to make a living as a writer.

By 1925, Hughes had established himself as a formidable poet, but he couldn't make a living at it full time. He took a job as a busboy at the Wardman Hotel in Washington, D.C., earning $55 a month. In November of 1925, a famous white poet, Vachel Lindsay, was giving a poetry reading in town. By chance, Lindsay happened to have dinner at the hotel where Hughes worked. It was precisely the opportunity the younger poet needed. Hughes placed several of his poems alongside the famous poet's plate.

Vachel Lindsay asked, "Who wrote this?"

"I did!" Hughes replied.

Lindsay was so impressed with the young poet's work, he made an announcement that very night that he had "discovered" a new young poet and read a handful of Hughes's poems to the excited audience. Newspapers throughout the United States picked up the story, which provided a considerable boost to Hughes's reputation. Langston Hughes went on to become one of the most important American poets of the twentieth century. His most famous poem, titled "Harlem," touches on themes of lost dreams, faded hopes, and a life of quiet desperation.

Lee Bennett Hopkins appreciated the sounds, rhythms, and the feel of Langston Hughes's poetry. Lee says, "[Langston Hughes] wrote about people I knew on city stoops and in city streets. Yet he captured those experiences—my experiences—in a few powerful words. It blew me away. It still does."

On the day that Langston Hughes died, May 22, 1967, Lee phoned Virginie Fowler, editor of children's books at Alfred A. Knopf, Inc., a New York City–based publishing company. He demanded to know why a new edition of Langston Hughes's poetry had not been published since 1932. The only existing edition of *The Dream Keeper* had badly outdated illustrations that were demeaning to African American men and women, and Lee refused to share that kind of book with his students.

The editor invited Lee out to lunch and suggested he edit a new book of Langston Hughes's poems. That sounded like a great idea to Lee, and he set to work on the project. Lee's new and improved edition, *Don't You Turn Back: Poems by Langston Hughes*, was published in 1969. He won an American Library Association's Notable Book Award and realized that he wanted to dedicate his life to poetry.

Many years later, the same publisher contacted Lee to ask if he would write the introduction for a new edition of Langston Hughes's *The Dream Keeper*, the very volume of poetry that had so inspired Lee nearly four decades earlier. In his introduction, Lee praised Hughes and admired his

Langston Hughes

James Langston Hughes was born in Joplin, Missouri, on February 1, 1902. Hughes was inspired by poets such as Paul Laurence Dunbar, Carl Sandburg, and Walt Whitman. His first book of poetry, *The Weary Blues*, was published in 1926. Besides poetry, Hughes wrote plays, short stories, and novels as well as newspaper articles and radio and television scripts.

lasting contributions to poetry. Lee wrote, "Little could [Langston Hughes] know that more than six decades after *The Dream Keeper* . . . first appeared in 1932, his passionate, sensitive, strong and mighty words would continue to be sung, shouted, whispered, hummed—from farmlands to suburbs, from cities to countrysides all over the world."

CIVIL RIGHTS MOVEMENT

While living in Harlem, Lee felt very much in his element. The kids in Harlem had known and felt all of the same kinds of joys and frustrations he felt growing up in Newark. The streets were vibrant, diverse, rich with life, but they could also be dangerous and unforgiving.

Lee recalls, "I looked around and saw children in the streets doing the same things that I did as a child. I suppose life doesn't change much when one is poor." He understood implicitly that many of the children in Harlem were struggling with the same troubles he had endured in his youth. Issues such as divorce, being raised by a single parent, and alcoholism were mostly kept private. Yet thousands of families, particularly

Some people rioted or destroyed property in Harlem in reaction to the assassination of Dr. Martin Luther King, Jr. in 1968.

those with young children, silently dealt with the pain and loss of broken families and dreams deferred.

Though Lee felt completely at home in Harlem, the death of Martin Luther King, Jr. changed the atmosphere in that part of the city. In 1968, at the height of his career, King was assassinated. Martin Luther King, Jr., the most important figure in the Civil Rights Movement during the 1950s and 1960s, inspired hundreds of thousands of African Americans to stand up for their rights as citizens of the United States of America. His death shocked the country, and life in Harlem became very unsettled. Lee felt compelled to leave, fearful of the potential for violence. He says, "The attitude of many black and white people in Harlem was becoming frightening as racial polarization became the norm and all whites were again an enemy. No matter what I knew or how I felt about these troubled times, I was *white*."

Lee left Harlem with an appreciation for the diversity of voices that needed to be presented to children throughout the United States,

Dr. Martin Luther King, Jr.

Born in Atlanta, Georgia, Dr. Martin Luther King, Jr. was a Baptist minister and social activist. He was an active force in the Civil Rights Movement from the mid–1950s until his untimely death. He helped orchestrate protests and boycotts against racial inequality. In 1964, he was awarded the Nobel Peace Prize for his work.

whether they lived in inner cities or posh suburbs. He became painfully aware of the ways that wonderful nonwhite poets were being excluded from classrooms.

To this day, Lee continues to remind readers how few poems by African American, Hispanic American, and Asian American writers are currently being discussed in schools. These poets have not been given the attention they deserve. It became a part of his mission, after leaving Harlem, to help more poets gain attention and find a well-deserved place in the classroom.

FIVE

Poetry and Imagination

Lee experimented with a number of innovative ideas in the classroom, but he noticed, above all, that young children responded to poetry at a profound level. Lee says, "I strongly believe that poetry should flow freely in our children's lives; it should come as naturally as breathing, for nothing—*no thing*—can ring and rage through our hearts and minds as does this body of literature." Unfortunately, schools were using the same old textbooks featuring the same predictable poets: Robert Louis Stevenson, Henry Wadsworth Longfellow, Robert Frost, and Carl Sandburg. When Lee was working in Harlem, he seized the opportunity to introduce his students to African American writers, such as Langston Hughes, Countee Cullen, and Gwendolyn Brooks. It occurred to him that other teachers might benefit from knowing more about his teaching techniques, so he wrote an article aimed at other grade-school teachers. His first professional essay was on the use of cinquain verse with children ("cinquain verse" is a five-line poem with a fixed number of syllables). He submitted it to a magazine called *Grade Teacher*. Not only did the magazine accept his article, the magazine featured it on the cover of one of its issues.

Lee wrote more and more articles, regularly publishing his work in professional magazines, such as *Horn Book*, *Instructor*, *Language Arts*, and others. Lee says, "I found that I could use poetry with almost every grade level, every age level. Vocabulary is usually simple. Poems are usually short. And I've always maintained that children can get more of an impact sometimes through eight or ten lines than they can in an entire novel. And my aim is to present it to them in an unthreatening way, so that they could develop a love of poetry and a love of language."

Lee wanted to change the way poetry was being taught to students. Many teachers presented poetry to their students as if it were some type of medicine that tasted bad.

The common theme that emerged in many of Lee's essays was a frustration with the ways that teachers incorporated poetry into classrooms, as if it were a tasteless but healthy vegetable that students should be forced to swallow. Lee perceived that teachers were interfering with poetry's power to uplift students. He studied the teaching and study guides many teachers relied on and found most of them counterproductive. They treated poetry like a science experiment, as if each poem should be dipped in formaldehyde and pinned down on its back in preparation for dissection. Too often, teachers allowed students one or two minutes to read a brief poem and then devoted the rest of the hour to a painstaking interpretation of the work. In that same period of time, the children could have read an entire volume of poetry.

Lee believes that children and young adults enjoy poetry best when it is experienced directly, through moods, emotions, and the power of rhythms. In his own words:

> What other form of literature could give me—give all of us— instant emotions to make us chuckle, weep, dance, or sigh—to bring those dreams to hold onto, those whispers, the melodious, mystifying, magic, and might of it all?

His professional essays emphasize the importance of nurturing children's emotional reactions to poetry. Lee warns teachers not to teach a poem unless they themselves absolutely fall in love with it. There are just too many poems in the world to choose from, so why should teachers and students waste time on poems they don't like?

He also explains that poetry for kids can be sophisticated. Poems about kittens, balloons, or ice cream can be lots of fun, but there ought to be room for poems that touch on deeper themes of love, hope, and the power of dreams. Poets such as T. S. Eliot, Wallace Stevens, and William Shakespeare can fit very comfortably into the classroom, as long as they are taught properly.

Many of Lee's beliefs stem from his own memories of elementary and high school. He hated school and found most of his classes incredibly boring. Lee recalls:

> I well remember hating Shakespeare as a high school student. I was forced to dissect, analyze, and memorize some fifteen isolated lines from *Julius Caesar*. . . . I soon came to detest the sound of the word

Lee knew that he could get students excited about poetry, even works by poets who were considered difficult to read, such as William Shakespeare.

poetry. It was not something to be enjoyed—it was a test of endurance and memorization ability.

As a young teenager, I wanted adventure, mystery, murder, passion. It wasn't until my adult years that I realized that Shakespeare . . . could have given me what I wanted then. Certainly the tragedies of Shakespeare dealt more passionately and romantically with life than did the drugstore magazines I bought with my weekly allowance. But I wasn't aware of this due to my sour poetic experiences.

Lee wants to teach children to love poetry, not to memorize and dissect it. He also believes in the power of reading poetry aloud. Reading aloud conveys a poem's rhythms, its mood, and even its silences. There's no reason readers shouldn't all walk around reciting words of poetry in their minds, in the same way they recite the lyrics to their favorite songs.

At the suggestion of a friend, Lee began to think about how he might present some of his teaching ideas in book form. He wrote up a sample chapter and an outline and submitted these to an editor at Scholastic Inc., a publisher of children's books and professional books for teachers. Within three weeks, an editor contacted Lee and told him to go ahead and write the book. His first professional book, called *Let Them Be Themselves: Language Arts Enrichment for Disadvantaged Children in Elementary Schools*, became enormously popular, selling more than 200,000 copies.

The editors at Scholastic were impressed with this young teacher and budding writer, and one afternoon in the spring of 1968, they called him into the Scholastic offices to offer him a job. They wanted him to work as a curriculum and editorial specialist, and because Lee knew that he had to leave Bank Street (and Harlem), he took the job almost immediately.

THE GRINCH AND THE WILD THINGS

In many ways, the job at Scholastic was the perfect opportunity for Lee at that point in his life. He could help teachers, promote authors, and work with poetry all day long. And it wasn't long before Lee crafted an exciting new book idea and proposed it to his fellow editors at Scholastic. Lee wanted to write a book filled with interviews of children's book authors and illustrators. He felt twenty-five interviews would make a nice little book and proposed the idea to his colleague, Mary L. Allison. Allison loved the idea, but she felt quite sure that twenty-five interviews wouldn't be enough. "Do one hundred or more," she suggested.

During the next several years, Lee compiled more than two hundred interviews with children's book authors and illustrators and published them as *Books Are by People* (1969) and *More Books by More People* (1974). Authors and illustrators discussed everything under the sun with Lee, from their work habits to their eating habits.

He interviewed legendary authors, such as E. B. White, author of *Charlotte's Web* and *Stuart Little*; Maurice Sendak, author of *Where the Wild Things Are* and *In the Night Kitchen*; and Beverly Cleary, author of the Ramona books. Even Dr. Seuss agreed to be interviewed for the collection.

Lee had an opportunity to share hot tea and toast with Maurice Sendak at his brownstone apartment in New York City's Greenwich Village. On entering Sendak's work studio, where he created the characters of Max and the wild things, Lee was struck by the author's walls. They were covered in books, newspaper clippings, pictures, toy pigs, lions, dogs, and various other animals. When asked about his work habits, Sendak replied, "When I write, I write sporadically, and I write everything in my head. My philosophy is, anything I forget should have been excluded."

The interview with Dr. Seuss was especially exciting for Lee. Many people had warned him about the difficulties of getting in touch with the famous author. Still, nothing was going to stop Lee from getting that interview. Despite his best efforts, Lee could not pin down a specific time for the two of them to meet. In a last-ditch

Maurice Sendak was one of the children's book authors featured in *Books Are by People*.

Meet Dr. Seuss

Dr. Seuss was born Theodor Seuss Geisel but was known to the world mostly by his pen name Dr. Seuss. His writing career is a great example of how being persistent can bring success. Dr. Seuss's very first book was turned down by more than twenty publishers. Most of the publishers complained that his stories and illustrations were too different from the norm.

Dr. Seuss wrote one of his best-selling books on the basis of a bet. His publisher, Bennett Cerf, bet Dr. Seuss that he couldn't write an entire book in just fifty words. Dr. Seuss took that bet and presented his publisher with a small masterpiece, *Green Eggs and Ham*.

attempt to get an interview, he mailed Dr. Seuss an in-depth questionnaire. The author finally found a few quiet moments to answer the questions—during his honeymoon in Reno, Nevada.

Lee learned that while Dr. Seuss's famous characters may seem whimsical, they were the product of intense labor. The author worked for months, sometimes years, to develop characters such as the Grinch, the Cat in the Hat, and Horton (Horton happened to be Dr. Seuss's favorite).

When Dr. Seuss began writing *The Cat in the Hat*, he expected it to take two to three weeks. Hardly! It ended up taking him well over a year. Dr. Seuss said, "To produce a 60-page book, I may easily write 1,000 pages before I'm satisfied. The most important thing about me, I feel, is that I . . . write, rewrite, reject, re-reject, and polish incessantly."

Dr. Seuss's comment echoes an idea that Lee Bennett Hopkins has put forth many times. Writing is work, hard work. It's not always easy and it's not always fun, but finishing a project is such a wonderful feeling that it makes all of the effort worthwhile.

THE BIRTH OF ANTHOLOGIES

At the same time Lee was working on *Books Are by People*, he also began to focus on the pressing need for more poetry anthologies in classrooms. Lee knew from his early years as a teacher in New Jersey that the kind of anthology he envisioned simply did not exist. He wanted teachers of history and math and science to incorporate poetry into their lessons, but no poetry collections existed on these subjects. Lee made it his mission to remedy that situation as quickly as he could. He planned to create anthologies on everything from astronomy to zoology so teachers in all fields could use poetry in their daily lessons.

When Lee prepares a new anthology, the first thing he does is come up with an idea for a topic. It may be a collection of poetry about baseball, math, science, or dinosaurs. Then he does a bit of preliminary research to see if the topic has been done before to avoid duplicating any books that already exist. He then searches for all of the poems he can find on that subject, which means browsing through hundreds of books in his own personal library, at the bookstore, or anywhere else he can find relevant works. He reads and rereads hundreds of poems, cutting down the list as much as he can until he finds exactly the right poems for his particular theme.

The work requires imagination and creativity, like an artist whittling wood or a sculptor shaping a beautiful form. Lee selects and discards just the right pieces until he finds the perfect tone, mood, and balance for each collection. He says:

> Balance is important in an anthology. I want many voices within a book, so I rarely use more than one or two works by the same poet. I also envision each volume as a stage play or film, having a definite beginning, middle, and end. The right flow is a necessity for me. Sometimes a word at the end of a work will lead into the title of the next selection. I want my collections to read like a short story or novel—not a hodgepodge of works thrown together aimlessly.

Lee tends to select serious poetry rather than light verse (light verse is a form of poetry that's usually humorous and rarely serious or profound) because he believes children get plenty of exposure to light verse through popular poets such as Shel Silverstein. He wants children to feel comfortable reading serious poets, such as Langston Hughes, Carl Sandburg, or William Shakespeare, as these authors can truly reveal the power and majesty of poetry.

TAKE-OUT POETS

Lee prides himself on including well-known, previously published poems alongside newly published works by contemporary authors. To get access to new, unpublished material, he has to be resourceful. Over time, Lee gained contacts with poets around the country and encouraged them to produce poems more or less on demand. He calls them his "take-out poets." He says, "There are several methods to my madness in pursuing these writers. One, it brings fresh voices to readers; second, it gives them the chance to become recognized and have their works reprinted. I am always on the search for new poetic talents because there are so few poets writing for children and I want to encourage as many as I can." If Lee is working on a particular theme, he will send these poets a topic, and they will produce new poems for his forthcoming collection.

For example, he wanted to build a collection of poetry around Stephen Alcorn's lovely woodcuts, after he and Stephen worked together on a previous book. He put his take-out poets to work. In this case, he sent every one of his poets an animal engraving by Alcorn. Each poet studied his or her animal drawing and used it for inspiration, and then

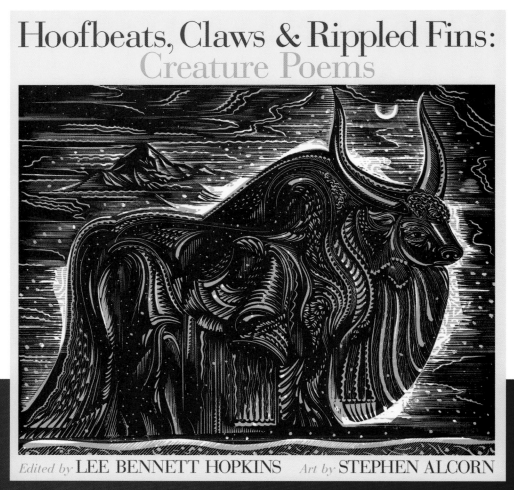

Hoofbeats, Claws & Rippled Fins:
Creature Poems

Edited by LEE BENNETT HOPKINS   *Art by* STEPHEN ALCORN

Lee and his take-out poets used Stephen Alcorn's artwork as inspiration for the poems in *Hoofbeats, Claws & Rippled Fins*.

composed a poem about it. The result was *Hoofbeats, Claws & Rippled Fins*, an award-winning collection.

Other times, he has an idea in his head for an anthology, and the raw material just does not exist, so he asks his poets to fill that void. For example, Lee wanted to put together a poetry anthology on dinosaurs. He did a great deal of research and found a number of poems about dinosaurs, mostly light verse, but they didn't fit the vision Lee had in his mind for this collection. He really wanted his dinosaur book to cover the entire time span of these fantastic creatures, from their early days ruling the earth to their extinction as a species. He commissioned his take-out poets to write eight new poems, and the resulting anthology on the history of dinosaurs fit his vision perfectly.

Lee's anthologies cover nearly everything an inspired classroom teacher could hope for. For the history teacher, he has assembled anthologies on American history and American geography. For the science

Miller-Brody Productions, Inc.

Presents...

pick a peck o' poems

A SOUND FILMSTRIP LIBRARY

By Lee Bennett Hopkins

This is a promotional flyer for a poetry filmstrip that Lee worked on. It was intended to "inspire young students to want to read, learn, and create their own poetry."

teacher, Lee has assembled anthologies on the seasons, weather, outer space, dinosaurs, bugs, and other creatures. There are also anthologies to celebrate holidays, birthdays, and, perhaps best of all, the joys of reading.

Lee even organized one of his anthologies by the length of each poem. In *Small Talk: A Book of Short Poems*, most of the poems have just two or three lines. *Small Talk* is a fun collection to read aloud that proves Lee's oft-stated belief that a well-formed poem can pack as much of an emotional punch in four lines as an entire novel.

Whatever the subject—science, math, sports, farm animals, holidays— Lee has a knack for bringing together poems that are both pleasing and profound. Lee says, "As an anthologist, I strive to bring the very best verse into children's lives. I want them to grow up on poetry, cherish it, make it a part of their being."

SIX

Birth of a Poet

Although it may seem that Lee Bennett Hopkins thinks about poetry exclusively within the classroom context, that could not be further from the truth. All those years surrounded by words, poems, and poets inspired him to try his own hand at writing. His very first poem was published in *Humpty Dumpty* magazine. The magazine paid him $15 to $20 per poem, which seemed like an awful lot of money to Lee at the time. He continued writing for small magazines until he had enough material to fill an entire volume.

In 1970, Lee published his own book of poetry called *This Street's For Me!*, which is filled with poems that reflect images from his vibrant and happy years living in Harlem. He says, "Many of the poems came right off these Harlem streets—the patter of the shoeshine boy, the sounds of the vendors, the feeling that something belongs to a child—in many cases a street."

Two years later, in 1972, Lee published a second collection of his own poetry called *Charlie's World.* "The poems in this book come from within me—from my own world, from my friends' world, from relatives," Lee says. "I wrote them over a long period of time and labored over each one. Charlie is a real person, and like the first poem in the book, he moved to a new apartment and has 'a room of his own / a room of his own / a room of his *own.*'" Whenever possible, Lee also includes his own poems in his anthologies.

This is Lee's thank-you letter to the college for naming him Outstanding Alumnus in the Arts.

TO: WILLIAM F. LOEHNING

FROM: LEE BENNETT HOPKINS

DATE: AUGUST 7, 1972

ON BEING NAMED OUTSTANDING ALUMNUS IN THE ARTS OF NEWARK STATE COLLEGE

Needless to say I am very pleased to be named an Outstanding Alumnus in the Arts of Newark State College. Without my basic education at Newark State College, my life certainly would not have been as rich as it has been. The memory of the college's credo has remained with me throughout my career: WHO DARES TO TEACH MUST NEVER CEASE TO LEARN. Teaching is one of the most complex professions that I know of but learning is "a profession" that must never end. Never.

This award is more than an honor to me. It is a statement—like the above credo. It says to me: Continue to learn, continue to teach, look back once in awhile, but only far enough to make you want to go ahead.

I sincerely thank the Alumni Association and all my colleagues at Newark State for this honor.

Some of Lee's early efforts drew a lot of attention from many different places, including his alma mater, Newark State College. In 1972, the college selected Lee as Outstanding Alumnus in the Arts. He was delighted to receive this honor and wrote the college a thank-you note that reflected on how his time at the school had shaped his life.

BRANCHING OUT

Lee continued to grow as a poet and found his work wonderfully satisfying. By 1976, he felt so passionate about his own writing career that he left his job at Scholastic in order to become a full-time writer.

He moved out of the city and found a home in a quiet, peaceful town in Westchester County, New York. Lee had never before lived in such a calming environment and could not believe how much his new home altered his outlook on the world. Believe it or not, he had never

A Special Anniversary

During the same year that Lee decided to pursue writing full time, the United States was celebrating the two hundredth anniversary of its independence. On July 4, 1976, numerous parades and other events were held across the country. New York City had its harbor filled with more than two hundred tall ships from around the world as part of its celebration.

quite realized that other birds existed in the world besides city pigeons. One day, a blue jay flew past his window, and he thought to himself, "It must be a blue pigeon. I thought, I didn't know they came in colors!"

He soon became aware of the changing seasons, of ducks and geese, bugs and butterflies, and all of the other pleasures of country living. His new home, surrounded by trees and flowers, felt very remote from the dark asphalt and gritty sidewalks of his youth.

Of course, he didn't become an overnight country boy. He still loves the thrill and excitement of New York City, only a forty-five-minute train ride away. And yet Lee's new home opened up a world of new images, sights, and smells.

Frequently, Lee gets an idea for a new poem based on his surroundings, perhaps something he has seen while walking. As you can imagine, a walk in downtown New York City will evoke radically different images than a walk through a lush flower garden or alongside a little stream.

The poems Lee wrote early on in his career focused on images drawn from city life, and they went something like this:

CITY BLOCKADES

I feel so small
standing beneath the tall
buildings that wall
me and the pigeons in

from the light of the
sky.

Notice how he has a reference to the city's pigeons. That single detail, the pigeons, helps to evoke an urban scene alongside the buildings so tall he can't even see the sunlight far above. Lee says that the inspiration for this poem came one day while walking around New York City. "I looked down at a pigeon pecking away. I looked up and felt surrounded, enveloped by steel."

A country poem, on the other hand, might go something like this:

CHANGE

When the first petals blow
the timeless stone wall
knows the reason:

Summer has grown old
ebbing toward
a sleep-time
season.

The "timeless" stone wall, blowing flower petals, and changing seasons evoke thoughts of New England farmhouses and sleepy towns. The details in this poem emphasize a slow, quiet pace: "timeless" stone, summer has "grown old," summer is "ebbing" and now it's "sleep-time." Far from the city's fast, frenetic pace, the poet takes time to stop and watch the slow, sleepy signs of a changing season.

Sometimes a small image, in combination with a particular event or experience, will inspire Lee to write a poem. When he took his dog to the veterinarian's office, for example, he wondered aloud whether the dog missed him as much as he missed his beloved dog. It's called "Overnight at the Vet's":

> *I found*
> *a strand*
> *of snow-white hair*
>
> *strewn upon his*
> *favorite chair*
>
> *I wonder how*
> *he's feeling there*
> *alone—*
>
> *I wonder*
> *if he wants*
> *his bone.*

I wonder
if he'll catch
a flea—

I wonder
if
he
misses
me.

It begins as a slightly mournful poem; the speaker finds a little tuft of dog fur and his thoughts soon wander to questions about his dog's state of mind. He obviously misses his dog badly. His final thought is made all that much more poignant by the spacing. If it just said, in a single line, "I wonder if he misses me," the question might seem offhand

Royal Dude

"Overnight at the Vet's" tells the story of the first night Lee's dog, Royal Dude, spent away from home. Royal Dude, a Cavalier King Charles spaniel, was a constant companion to Lee for many years. Lee says that Dude's death was one of the saddest times for him and still wonders ". . . if he misses me."

and casual. But to give each single word its own line forces the reader to slow down and really grasp the poet's feelings of loneliness.

Lee began to include many of his own poems in the dozens of poetry anthologies he published over the years. He wrote poems anywhere and everywhere: on trains, on planes, even in the car. "What's wonderful about being a writer," he says, "is that you don't know what's going to happen tomorrow, you don't know what's going to spark you." A pad of paper and pencil accompanied him wherever he went so he would always be prepared when inspiration hit.

Although Lee loved the challenge of writing individual poems, strong and vivid memories of his childhood crept back into his mind and inspired him to take on a completely new challenge: a full-length novel.

TELLING HIS STORY

In 1977, Lee published his first young adult novel called *Mama*. He originally conceived of the project in rather modest terms—as a brief picture book—but his editor, Pat Ross, suggested that the book might work best as a full-length novel. Lee was taken aback. He had written plenty of poems, numerous essays, and even full-length professional books for teachers, but a novel sounded a bit intimidating.

Nevertheless, the idea grew on him, and he set to work right away. In the 1970s, personal computers did not exist. Lee sat down with a pen and paper and composed his notes, which eventually were transformed into chapters. Before long, the chapters coalesced into a full draft. Because the entire manuscript consisted of handwritten pages, it wasn't especially easy to make revisions. He frequently cut entire sections away with scissors and pasted them into other parts of the manuscript to get the flow of the story exactly how he wanted it.

The novel *Mama* details many of Lee's childhood experiences. It tells the story of a bold, brash, and hard-working mother who raises her two sons the best way she knows how. She steals, talks her way out

This is the front cover of the first edition of *Mama*.

of tight spots, and asks her oldest son to participate in many of her escapades.

Mama holds a special place in Lee's heart because he feels that its main character becomes more and more relevant to kids' lives every passing year. He says, "Today there are more single-parent mothers than ever before—women who struggle to juggle long hours at workplaces, raise children, try hard to cope with a multitude of life problems."

His favorite quote from the novel comes from a concerned neighbor named Mrs. Rand. She says, "Lovin' has the power to change things. It can change this whole, wide, sometimes confusin' world." Mama might have made several bad choices in her struggle for survival, but she always shows unconditional love to her sons, and that is enough to change her sons' lives for the better.

After *Mama*, Lee published two more novels. His second novel, *Wonder Wheels* (1979), is the story of Mick Thompson and Kitty Rhoades, a teenage couple who share a love of roller skating. The couple fall in love, but Kitty continues to be harassed by her ex-boyfriend. The story is based on Lee's teenage relationship with Evelyn.

In 1981, Lee returned to his beloved, semiautobiographical character of Mama and wrote a sequel called *Mama and Her Boys*. It has the same cast of characters, but this time, the story focuses on Mama's desire to marry her boss, Mr. Jacobs. Her two sons would prefer that she marry the school janitor, Mr. Carlisle.

In all of his writing drawn from his life, Lee tries to show youngsters they are not alone, that many children experience the pain of

An Honorary Doctor

In 1980, Lee received an honorary doctorate from Kean University, making him a Doctor of Laws. Today, while maintaining its commitment to train teachers, Kean University has expanded its offerings to forty-five undergraduate and twenty-six graduate degree programs.

divorce, money problems, and family conflicts. Children can get through these difficult times and come out strong.

THE REAL MAMA

While his fictionalized account of his life with his mother achieved great success, Lee's relationship with the real "Mama" remained complicated. As an adult, Lee found his mother to be as delightful and confusing as ever. He loved his mother but could never understand why she seemed to be so unhappy. He thought that her drinking problem may have been a factor.

Lee shares a close moment with his mother during one of their holiday celebrations.

Lee's mother could be wonderful, and she could be critical. To friends, family, and anyone else she met, she would rave about her successful son, calling him the "biggest and most famous author in the world." However, she never did share her joy about her son's success with Lee directly. While she knew that he was an accomplished writer and anthologist, she didn't completely understand his career. "Did you ever think about getting a real job?" she would ask.

Despite her problems, Lee's mother remained an important force in Lee's life. While she may not have voiced her support for him, she showed her love for him by participating in events that mattered to him. While attending a luncheon honoring Lee, she met Lee's longtime agent, Marilyn E. Marlowe. Marlowe described Lee's mother as "vivacious, attractive, and totally enthralled by her son."

Pleasant *Surprises*

Lee continued to receive positive responses to his work. In 1984, Lee's poetry collection entitled *Surprises* was published. The book is the first poetry book in the I Can Read series intended for beginning readers. The collection was selected as one of the best books of the year by *School Library Journal* and as a notable book by the American Library Association. It also made the Texas Bluebonnet Award List.

The 1980s were a time of great success and wondrous surprises for Lee.

SEVEN

Extra Innings

The success of Lee's career is based, in part, on the challenges he overcame in his childhood. Poetry changed his life, but it also sprang from the story of his life. And yet, one question still roamed in the back of Lee's mind: What had become of his father? When Leon walked out on the family, none of the children ever expected to see him again. Lee's sister, Donna Lea, remembered virtually nothing about the man. She was only three years old when he left.

As it turns out, Leon had tried to get in touch with his children numerous times, but he could never track them down. They moved around too much, often skipping out on the rent when money ran low, with no forwarding address left behind. So Lee's father moved on with his life too.

Lee and his siblings had a joyous reunion with their father in 1985.

In 1985, more than three decades after Leon had left his family behind in Newark, he received a phone call out of the blue. On the other end of the line was the daughter he barely knew, Donna Lea, and she wanted to see him. He was thrilled to hear from her, and they quickly organized a reunion.

After all those years, Lee and Donna Lea did not know what to expect. Their father lived in California and had never remarried. That's all they knew about him.

The reunion was a joyful success. Leon was extremely proud of his son, the poet. He would walk into the local public library and brag about Lee Bennett Hopkins, the famous author. For his part, Lee felt very tender and loving toward his father. Lee says, "My father's coming back into our lives was one of the most moving experiences of my life. Those were rich years."

When Leon passed away, just four years after the reunion, Lee dedicated one of his anthologies to him. The book, a collection of poetry about baseball, was called *Extra Innings: Baseball Poems*. In the dedication, Lee thanked his father for the "extra innings" they were able to share together.

HIGH PRAISE

When Lee won the University of Southern Mississippi Medallion in 1989, he joined some prestigious company. Past award winners include Ezra Jack Keats, Jean Fritz, Madeleine L'Engle, and Maurice Sendak. The university has been giving out this award every year since 1969 for outstanding contributions in the field of children's literature. People from the education and publishing fields submit nominations for the award, and a committee of authors, librarians, and experts in children's literature

Good Rhymes, Good Times!

In 1985, a collection of Lee's original poetry, *Good Rhymes, Good Times!*, was published. One poem from that collection, "Good Books, Good Times!," has special meaning for Lee. It was chosen as the 1985 Children's Book Week Poem. "In many ways the verse sums up all I feel about the love I have for children, for educators, for parents, for teachers and librarians who do, indeed, enrich our children's lives with 'Good books / good times. . .'"

vote for the winner from the list of nominations. The committee takes into account the author's entire body of work.

Three silver medallions bearing the likeness of the author are made for the winner, the president of the university, and for the de Grummond Children's Literature Collection's permanent display. Today, the de Grummond Collection houses the Lee Bennett Hopkins Papers. The papers include autobiographical and biographical materials, correspondence,

Side by Side

About a year before Lee won the University of Southern Mississippi Medallion, his anthology *Side by Side: Poems to Read Together* was published. In the book, Lee brought a mixture of classic and contemporary children's poems into one collection. It featured the work of Lewis Carroll, Robert Louis Stevenson, and Robert Frost. The illustrations were done by Hilary Knight, perhaps best known as the illustrator of the Eloise books.

and some of his books in different stages of production. Researchers can review Lee's original manuscripts and see what changes may have been made later in the process, such as after he reviewed the galleys or the typeset pages of the books.

NURTURING TALENT

Poetry enriches people's lives, fills their hearts with emotion, and sparks their imaginations, but poetry rarely brings riches to its writers. It can be very difficult for poets to establish themselves and gain enough recognition to make a living as full-time writers.

Lee wanted to encourage all of his fellow poets to keep writing, so in 1993, he established the Lee Bennett Hopkins Poetry Award. It is a national award honoring a children's author or anthologist for a single volume of poetry. In recognition of his hometown of Scranton, Pennsylvania, Lee asked the Children's Literature Council of Pennsylvania to

Lee poses with Nancy Wood, one of the winners of the Lee Bennett Hopkins Poetry Award.

sponsor the award, which they happily agreed to do. The award is now administered by Pennsylvania State University.

Every year, the organization contacts publishers across the United States, inviting them to submit an outstanding poetry collection for consideration. A committee reviews all of the submissions, usually somewhere between sixty and one hundred books, until it finds a winner. Other books may be cited as honor books. While Lee does not take part in the process of review or final selection, he does donate the $500 award, and his name appears on the distinctive seal that marks every prize-winning book. The seal features Jesse Wilcox Smith's illustration of Mother Goose with a small child under each wing and the words "The Lee Bennett Hopkins Poetry Award."

In addition, Lee sponsors the Lee Bennett Hopkins/International Reading Association Promising Poet Award, which is presented every three years. The award honors poets who have published at least one book of poetry but no more than two.

Ever since Lee first discovered the power of poetry, he has been committed to the importance of sharing and teaching diverse

This is the official seal of the Lee Bennett Hopkins Poetry Award.

Advice to Young Poets

When asked what advice he has for young poets, the first thing Lee says is that good writers are readers. If you want to write poetry, read the best poetry. If you want to write mystery novels, read the best mysteries. Reading the works of others helps you find your own voice as a writer.

It is also important to be observant. Look at the world with a writer's eye. That's not just seeing but hearing, smelling, touching, and tasting too. Ask questions. Remember details. Keep a notebook of your observations, and you'll find you'll always have things to write about.

Remember that writing is not always easy, and you shouldn't expect that it will be. Much of writing can be rewriting, working with words until they sound just right. The pleasure and pride you can feel at the results are worth the effort.

poetic voices. Too often, the school curriculum is defined by white male poets, with less attention paid to women, African Americans, Asian Americans, and other minority groups. Just as Lee was entirely committed to the magnificent poetry of Langston Hughes, he has continued to nurture and seek out less-well-known poets. The Lee Bennett Hopkins poetry awards allow him to bring forward new, fresh, promising poetic voices. Perhaps another Langston Hughes is out there, waiting to be discovered.

POETIC GUIDE TO HISTORY

Lee gave readers another way to approach history with his 1994 collection entitled *Hand in Hand: An American History Through Poetry*. The collection

BEEN TO YESTERDAYS

Poems of a Life
by LEE BENNETT HOPKINS

A picture of a teenage Lee appears on the cover of *Been to Yesterdays*, a collection of Lee's poetry about his early life.

is a poetic melting pot of historic, contemporary, and new voices, ranging from E. B. White to Prince Redcloud. These poets take the reader from the 1600s to the twenty-first century by way of different eras and themes.

The book is divided into nine sections. Each section covers a different theme, event, or historical period and opens with a brief introduction that sets the stage for the poetry featured in the section.

That same year, Lee took a whimsical approach to the alphabet with *April Bubbles Chocolate*. The alphabet is created by the first letter in the title of each poem. One critic described it as "another fine effort by this reliable anthologist."

POETRY CLOSE TO HOME

Lee returned to the source of much of his writing—his personal experiences—with *Been to Yesterdays: Poems of a Life*

(1995). In that collection, he recounts many of the memorable moments from his middle-school years: moving from place to place, memories of his beloved grandmother, his parents' divorce. Lee's experiences as a youth were difficult, but the book ends on a note of hope. Lee resolves to "make the world a whole lot brighter" by becoming a writer.

He dedicated the collection to "four unique mothers"—his own, Elizabeth M. Brown, Bernice E. Cullinan, and Elizabeth Isele. Brown, Cullinan, and Isele were all editors for Boyds Mills Press, the company that published the book. Cullinan described Lee as taking "storytelling and poetry to a new level."

Lee wrote *Been to Yesterdays* to send a message to all children that they can survive the rough times with hope. He takes pride in the fact that he survived his childhood with the love of his mother, the gift of hope from Mrs. McLaughlin, and a promise to himself that he would be strong and make a difference in children's lives. He says:

> With love and encouragement each of us can get through tough times. We have all been to our own yesterdays. It is the tomorrows that count; the future—the future of all young people who must be instilled with a strong self-concept for brighter days ahead.

The book struck a chord with both children and critics alike. *Been to Yesterdays* won the Christopher Book Award in 1996. The Christopher Awards are given to people in several different categories in media, such as books, films, and television, who create works that "affirm the highest values of the human spirit." *Been to Yesterdays* went on to receive numerous awards.

A SENSE OF PLACE

Lee came up with the idea of pairing poetry with factual information in *My America: A Poetry Atlas of the United States* (2000). Accompanied by rich, colorful illustrations by Stephen Alcorn, this book takes the reader on a journey across the United States through verse. The book is divided into eight sections, each covering a different region of the country. Each section opens with a map pointing out the state capitals in the region and a table of facts, such as the state flower and size of the state, on each state covered. Including the facts along with the poems presents the reader with an interesting opportunity to learn specific information about each state and enjoy one poet's interpretation of the same place.

Famous *Lives*

After writing about his own life, Lee worked on a collection that would tell young readers about the lives of many important people. Published in 1999, *Lives: Poems about Famous Americans* profiles a variety of people in verse, from Sacagawea to Babe Ruth. Rather than going over sometimes tedious facts about a person, the poems provide a glimpse of the spirit of the subject, such as David Bouchard's "Walt Whitman." Bouchard's poem portrays Whitman as a man of great vision.

Lee himself tackles an interesting mix of states and one state capital, from "Kentucky" to "Wisconsin in Feb-b-rr-uary" to "Seattle Morning." He says in his introduction, "*My America* depicts our always forever-changing land. Through poets' voices our senses are stirred, shaken, awakened to witness the various regions that make up our great United States."

Working again with Alcorn, Lee also took a more personal approach to places with *Home to Me* (2002). In his editor's note, Lee says, "Where we live—the place we call home—strongly influences our way of life." Each poet in the collection has written about what home is to him or her, resulting in a mosaic of American life. Joseph Bruchac's "Rez Road" explores living on a reservation while Lee's own "City I Love" takes the reader through a city day from morning through nightfall.

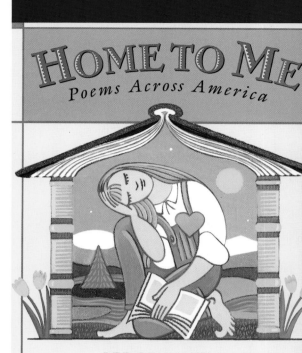

HOME TO ME
Poems Across America

Selected by LEE BENNETT HOPKINS
Illustrated by STEPHEN ALCORN

Home to Me once again paired Lee with illustrator Stephen Alcorn.

Lee enjoys reading some poetry during a quiet moment at home.

EIGHT

Today and Tomorrow

For Lee, not a day goes by without poetry. Whether it's writing, reading, or assembling poems for an anthology, poetry always stands at the center of his life. Lee says, "Poetry and I fit together. I can't imagine life without it. Were it in my power, I would give poetry to every single child everywhere. What it can do for life and lives is magical. It is food and drink. It is the seasons. It is the stuff of all existence. How rich my life has been because of the genre. How rich it can be for everyone."

Lee works in a study and library on the second floor of his home. Its walls are covered in books, thousands of books, creating an impressive home library. In the middle of his study sits his desk, orderly and

A Fan of Beauty

Lee does not need to look out his window to see beauty. He can simply walk around his home and view wonderful works of art. Lee's home contains numerous pieces of art that he has collected over the years during his travels. Several life-sized sculptures can be found throughout his home.

inviting, with a window looking out onto the lordly Hudson River. He often jokes that the view is so lovely, he must face his chair away from the window when trying to get work done or it will distract him from the task at hand. At other times, the river's beauty and majesty inspire him to write.

Lee doesn't have a set routine each day, which is perhaps a carryover from his youth, when he learned to detest fixed rules and routines. He doesn't feel the need to structure each minute of every day, and he simply writes when he feels like it. And yet, he's very disciplined, often working on several projects at a time. It's a varied and ever-changing lifestyle, just the way he likes it.

When Lee sits down to work on a poem, it doesn't necessarily evolve exactly as he might have planned. Some poems come to him all at once, and he simply writes them down. Most take months and months of writing and revision. In fact, Lee once quipped, "Sometimes I think there's no such thing as writing. There's only re-writing." And then there are some poems that never get finished at all.

Every stage of writing requires work. First, Lee is struck by an interesting idea. He puts the first words on the page. Then he revises, revises, and revises again until the words sound just right. Lee says, "If there is one message I could send to young writers it's that writing is hard, needs to be reworked, and is a skill that takes time to be perfected." He never knows what will come easily and what will take weeks or months, but he keeps at it until the words flow together and he's happy with it. If he reads his own poem and says, "OOOOH!" then he knows the work on

Lee works at his desk in his upstairs office. He never knows how long it will take him to write a poem.

it is finally done. The process can be difficult and draining at times, but the end result offers such a deep sense of satisfaction that Lee goes back for more every single day.

Lee was once asked, "What if you don't know what to write about?" He answered the question this way:

> You always have something to write about if you start with what you know. Perhaps you live near a river. What's that river like? Does it change with the weather? With the seasons? How did the river get its name? Think about what you know and capture the images and the details that come to mind in words.
>
> That works with anything—baseball, a friend, a tree in your backyard. Go take a look at your tree before you try to write. Look

Lee reviews his original poem for the letter *C* for his book *Alphathoughts*.

for animals and insects living in it. Smell the tree and feel its bark. Talk about that tree with someone. It will help the words begin to flow.

Lee is a whirlwind of creative energy and is usually working on several different book projects at the same time. One of Lee's recent projects was *Alphathoughts*. He wrote a poem for each letter of the alphabet, and each title begins with the featured letter. The featured letter can be also found in one of the lines of the poem. The result is another delightful collection of simple and appealing poetry. In the words of one critic, "Hopkins's poetry says a lot in just a few words."

Lee has been a full-time writer for more than twenty-five years now, and he shows no signs of slowing down. He gets so many ideas for new poems and poetry collections that he must use entire filing cabinets to keep track of them all. Whether it's an idea for a book or a single poem, he writes it down. The cabinets are quite full, so it appears that Lee will be busy for years to come.

A PRESENT FOR THE FUTURE

Though Lee has reached an age at which many people consider retirement, he continues to work as hard as ever. His endless energy and passion for life make him seem ageless. His intuitive understanding of poetry and its importance in the school curriculum have made him a very popular speaker at professional meetings and conferences around the country. Through his lectures and workshops, Lee continues to educate teachers about the significance of sharing poetry with children every single day in every area of the curriculum. His message has transformed classrooms around the nation and created lifelong poetry fans. In his own words:

> Give children poetry—a gift from the past, a present for the future—words and thoughts and feelings they will remember, thank you for, their whole lives through.

Lee also continues to produce new books. His list of publications already tops one hundred, but he knows there are more books to be written, and he still gets a thrill when one of his books first shows up in print. He says, "Opening the bound copy for the first time is like seeing

Lee checks the page proofs for one of his upcoming books.

the big curtains being raised in a darkened theater. It's magical, fun, scary." If it is a book he loves (and he doesn't love them all), he picks it up and carries it around with him for a few days. Then, he puts the new book down and rarely looks at it again. Lee has so many new projects he still wants to write, there is little time to dwell on the past.

And perhaps that best captures the spirit of Lee Bennett Hopkins. Live in the present. Work on the future. Be happy now. Embrace love. With his glimmering eyes and bright smile, he loves to laugh and effortlessly exudes his enthusiasm for reading, poetry, and life itself. Yesterday may have been full of sorrows, but today is filled with potential.

Timeline

1980 Lee receives a honorary doctor of laws degree from Kean University.

1985 Lee and his siblings reunite with their father.

1989 Lee is awarded the University of Southern Mississippi Medallion. Lee receives Keystone State (Pennsylvania) Author of the Year Award.

1993 The first Lee Bennett Hopkins Poetry Award is presented.

1995 The first Lee Bennett Hopkins/International Reading Association Promising Poet Award is presented.

1996 Lee wins a Christopher Award for *Been to Yesterdays*.

To Find Out More

SELECTED BOOKS WRITTEN OR EDITED BY LEE BENNETT HOPKINS

Alphathoughts: Alphabet Poems from A to Z. Honesdale, PA: Boyds Mills Press, 2003.

Been to Yesterdays. Honesdale, PA: Boyds Mills Press, 1995.

Blast Off! Poems about Space. New York: HarperCollins, 1995.

Climb into My Lap: First Poems to Read Together. New York: Simon & Schuster, 1998.

Easter Buds Are Springing: Poems for Easter. Honesdale, PA: Boyds Mills Press, 1993.

Good Rhymes, Good Times!: Original Poems. New York: HarperCollins, 1995.

Hand in Hand: An American History Through Poetry. New York: Simon & Schuster, 1994.

Home to Me: Poems Across America. New York: Orchard Books, 2002.

Hoofbeats, Claws & Rippled Fins: Creature Poems. New York: Harper-Collins, 2002.

Lives: Poems about Famous Americans. New York: HarperCollins, 1999.

Mama. Honesdale, PA: Boyds Mills Press, 2000.

Mama and Her Boys. Honesdale, PA: Boyds Mills Press, 2000.

Marvelous Math: A Book of Poems. New York: Simon & Schuster, 1997.

My America: A Poetry Atlas of the United States. New York: Simon & Schuster Books for Young Readers, 2000.

Pass the Poetry, Please! New York: HarperCollins, 1998.

Pauses: Autobiographical Reflections of 101 Creators of Children's Books. New York: HarperCollins, 1995.

School Supplies: A Book of Poems. New York: Simon & Schuster, 1996.

Small Talk: A Book of Short Poems. New York: Harcourt Brace, 1995.

Song and Dance: Poems. New York: Simon & Schuster, 1997.

Spectacular Science: A Book of Poems. New York: Simon & Schuster, 1999.

Sports! Sports! Sports!: A Poetry Collection. New York: HarperCollins, 1999.

Wonderful Words. New York: Simon & Schuster, 2004.

The Writing Bug. Katonah, NY: Richard C. Owen, 1993.

ORGANIZATIONS AND ONLINE SITES

Children's Book Council "Meet the Author"
http://www.cbcbooks.org/html/lbhopkins.html

This site includes a brief note from Lee Bennett Hopkins about the importance of poetry in his career.

**International Reading Association/
Lee Bennett Hopkins Promising Poet Award
http://www.reading.org/awards/Lee.html**

This site is dedicated to the Promising Poet Award and includes a list of past winners.

**Lee Bennett Hopkins Is Still the Little Kid from Newark
http://www.teachingk-8.com/archives/html/1_99outtakes1.html**

This site features an article from *Teaching K–8* about Hopkins that provides a brief overview of his career.

**Lee Bennett Hopkins Papers
http://lib.usm.edu/%7Edegrum/html/research/findaids/hopkins.htm**

The University of Mississippi de Grummond Collection houses a variety of documents related to Hopkins's work, including autobiographical materials, typescripts, correspondence, and compilations of poetry.

**Lee Bennett Hopkins Teacher Resource File
http://falcon.jmu.edu/~ramseyil/hopkins.htm**

This site contains biography, bibliography, lesson plans, criticism, and awards in honor of Lee Bennett Hopkins.

A Note on Sources

This biography would not have been possible without the existence of two crucial sources. First, Lee's detailed autobiographical essay in Something About the Author Autobiography series, and second, my own series of conversations with Lee Bennett Hopkins himself. Lee generously agreed to give numerous interviews for this biography, occasionally covering personal territory that he hadn't thought about in years. In addition, he kindly sent me a packet of publicity materials, interviews, and essays about his life and work.

I also consulted many published interviews and articles about Lee Bennett Hopkins. A few titles in the Something About the Author series were particularly helpful. Some of the articles I found most useful include: "Special Interview," *Phonics Today*; "Profile: Lee Bennett Hopkins," *Language Arts*, Nov/Dec 1978; "Making Kids Well-Versed in Poetry," *Suburban People*, 15 Jan. 1989; "A Visit With Lee Bennett Hopkins," *Journal of the Children's Literature Council of Pennsylvania*, vol. 6, no. 2, 1992; "A Conversation with Lee Bennett Hopkins," *Book Links*, July 1994; "Conversations: Lee Bennett Hopkins," *The Five Owls*, March/April 1996; "Books Remembered," *CBC Features*, spring 1997; "Lee Bennett Hopkins' Poetry Speaks to Young People," *Curriculum Administrator*, Nov/Dec 1997; "Interview," *Teaching K–8*, January 1999; and "A Passion for Poetry," *Teacher Librarian*, June 2000.

—*Amy Strong*

Index

About the Author

Amy Strong earned a Ph.D. in twentieth-century American literature from the University of North Carolina at Chapel Hill. She has written and published essays on several of her favorite authors, including Ernest Hemingway, William Faulkner, Toni Morrison, and Virginia Woolf. She lives in the great state of Maine with her husband, Dave, and their golden retriever, Jamison.